All I'm Becoming

All I'm Becoming

Rozemarijn van Kampen

Writer: Rozemarijn van Kampen
Cover design: Rozemarijn van Kampen
ISBN: 9789403632216

Foreword

I've written these poems in the span of about 1,5 to 2 years. I have changed a lot in this period, and so did my feelings. Some of the poems I have written, are not how I see myself anymore. However, they are still part of me and part of my journey. That is why I want to share them with you.

This book is divided in three chapters. Each is about a different aspect of my life: hurt, love, and growth. They each tell a story of the things I've experienced, the things I've learned, and the things I'm ready to move on to. The poems do not rhyme, they are based on my feelings, the way the words felt right to me.

Not everyone may agree with my style, and not everyone may understand my words, but don't worry about that. I appreciate the fact that you've taken the time to read this book.

Content Warning

This work contains the following topics that you may feel uncomfortable with.

- Sexual Assault
- Rape
- Self-Harm
- Depression
- Death
- Suicide
- Body dysmorphia
- Capitalism

Be gentle with yourself. I will do the same.

I want to thank Alex, for believing in me and helping me become who I am now.

I want to thank Zoë for always being there for me, even when we don't speak for months.

I want to thank Yente for encouraging me to go further and for helping me realize how queer I am.

I want to thank my family for always supporting me, no matter what I do and what I choose. Thanks to you, I can be who I am.

Special thanks to Valeria Eden, author of "I used to be the sun". Because of her book and tweets, I was inspired to put my own feelings on paper as well.

And lastly,
I want to thank all my twitter mutuals. I may not know you personally, I may not know your lives, but you support me and accept my regular rants online.

I hope you all enjoy this book. It's a piece of me I'm giving away in good faith. Take good care of it.

Content

All that hurt

Sunlight hits my face
I can feel the warm kisses on my freckles
Hot air in my lungs
I flourish

Rain hits my face
I can feel its tears running down my cheeks
Smell of petrichor in my nose
I grow

Walls surround me
I can feel the appliances' electricity surrounding me
Anxious thoughts wash over me
I wither

People pass me by
I can feel their collective energy filling my head
Pain stabs me in my bowels
I cry

I was not made for this society

I was nine
Sat on the toilet
Praying
Wishing better for the world

Easter came
Christian school, Jesus rises, the works
God didn't exist
He didn't help the world

My world shattered
Crying in my mother's arms
This wasn't in the parent handbook
I called in sick

Trying on clothes
You shouldn't
Putting on makeup
Why would you?

Minding my business
I hate you
Taking pictures
You're pathetic

Crying
You're worthless
Scratching my face
You should kill yourself

Ruining my relationship
You deserve it
Looking for a way out
Good

Seeking help
...
Talking to a therapist
...

Getting treatment
...
Getting send home
...
Home
Did you miss me?

-    Depression is a bitch

I feel

I feel and I think, but I can't understand.

I rationalize. I need to find meaning. When I can't, I repeat. I repeat. I repeat. I repeat.

I think

I think and I feel, but I can't comprehend

I cry. What am I feeling? What am I feeling? What am I feel…? What am I?

I can't recognize my feelings
They call it alexithymia

To me, feelings are like a faded memory
A glimpse of meaning
Always just out of reach

And when I try to grab it
It trickles through my fingers
As if I were holding sand

The first time I saw a therapist as an adult
She grabbed the DSM-5 booklet
Checked all the symptoms I explained
And told me I had depression
As if I didn't already know

When I talked to her about my anxiety
My bowels, my panic attacks, and breakdowns
She disregarded them
And made me do a task I could not complete
As if I were just another statistic

When I met her colleague for evaluation
I told her I didn't feel like therapy was working
That they used the wrong kind
She told me I just had to be patient
And called my boyfriend an old dude

- Cognitive Behavioral Therapy, my ass

Undiagnosable
At least, that's how I see myself
When I suffered from depression
I got the diagnosis until another disorder came into view

They presumed I was autistic
I checked all the boxes
My mother did too
It could be inherited

When I got the results
They told me I was too social
I checked all the boxes
But I lived my life too well to get the official diagnosis

They told me I had alexithymia
But only if I succeeded
Doing special therapy
Otherwise, I may be autistic after all

They told me they couldn't label me as depressed
Since my potential autism could explain my feelings
But I can't be labeled autistic
Since I "function" too well

Undiagnosable

We're all victims of capitalism
Puppets in the hands of billionaires
You get born into the world
With an unwanted subscription on life
Costs: expensive

You work because you need to pay your bills
You need to pay your bills to get housing
You need housing to be seen as human
Rather than as a dirty beggar

When you can't work
You are lazy
When you're ill
You're a burden

If you can't pay your bills
You lose everything

When you want to leave the system
You need to be rich or you won't make it

You can work hard to achieve your dreams
But you'll lose a few decades of your life in the process

I used to be outside for hours
Broken shoes
Ripped jeans
Not a care in the world

Nearly every year we went to France
A camping ground neighboring a lake
There was absolutely nothing there
Yet it was my second home

Nature calls to me
Wants me home
Yet, here I am
Stuck in a concrete city

I am inside for hours
Laptop screen
Iced coffee
Stressed out of my mind

Not enough money to move
To start life elsewhere
Connect with nature again
Feeling normal again

I would still write
But I would also paint
Garden
Sing
Cook
And Hike

Just living life like I was meant to be

Sometimes
On a dark day

Words swirl around in my head
Like a raging storm
Unwilling to calm

Tears stream down my cheeks
Like waterfalls
Desperately trying to reach the ground

My nails digging into my skin
Creating trenches
Making holes to plot new soil

I am a world trying to destroy itself

It's easier to please others than to put yourself first

When I was 16, I wasn't depressed.
Everyone wants to be dead sometimes.
Everyone thinks out a plan to kill themselves and
everyone has written a suicide-note telling their family it
is not their fault.
No, I wasn't depressed, I was just sad, like all teenagers
are sometimes. It's what my doctor said.

When I was 16, I wasn't depressed.
I probably just scratched my arms till the marks stayed
visible because I wanted attention.
I clawed at my head, crying hysterically because I was
being dramatic.
I drew out ways to die, wrote texts about wanting to die
in a private notebook to stay "edgy".
I wasn't depressed.

When I was 19, I wasn't depressed.
It was just a winter-dip.
It would all be over soon.
Those episodes in which I screamed and cried and
wanted to die would all be over soon once spring came.
It is not a depression, I've had this before, when I was
16.
Don't worry, it will go away.

It didn't go away

I'm sorry, I say
What for? He asks
Everything.

I apologize too much
For feeling depressed
For forgetting about a non-important grocery item
For sleeping in a little too late

I'm sorry, I say
For forgetting to do the dishes
Or not closing the window when the mosquitoes come in
For missing a kiss he leaned in for

I'm sorry, I repeat
For saying something negative about myself
For not wanting to have sex
And for putting his clothes in the hamper when he
wanted to continue wearing them

I apologize for everything
From forgetting to water the plants
To having emotions
To having a physical body in this world

I'm sorry, I say
For existing

It's sad that the only times I feel normal
Is when I use drugs

It's sad that when I told my doctor
She ignored my concerns and talked over me

It's sad that I know exactly how much and when to take it
To prevent addiction and tolerance

It's sad that I only use it to work
When people my age use it to party

It's sad that I need to self-medicate with illegal drugs
Just because the system doesn't want to diagnose me

To:
The man on the train who masturbated while watching
me after which he walked by and gave me the signal for
fingering women
The man who kept insisting I needed to come over so he
could help me with my homework when I was 12
The men that kept following my best friend and I after we
declined their offer to go to a club
The man that harassed multiple women on the subway
and grabbed his cock as he walked past my window
The boy that kept sexually harassing my best friend
The boy that she considered to be her close friend
The boys I thought were my friends
The man that implied blackmail when I didn't want to
sext with him
The men that wrote out their physically abusive fantasies
about me and send them to me
The men that have catcalled to me, to my friends, to all
women
The men that have harassed and catcalled my sisters or
will do so in the future

Fuck you!
Fuck you!

Women do not owe you anything
Women do not exist for your pleasure
Women deserve respect
We are not your objects.

Sometimes my mind and body are restless
Never enough, always too much
My fingers stop, my legs won't work, and my mouth
stays closed

Everything I love
Everything I used to do
Useless and empty

All this pent up energy
With no way out
Just staring at my screen for hours

Unfinished work
New projects
It just doesn't feel right

My therapist called me a computer
Highly intelligent
But with an oh so low processor speed

Open one too many tabs?
I'll freeze completely
Start a task but change your mind?
404

The messages, the ads, the people
Where is that music coming from?
Everything is so fast and so loud
I don't understand

I may not understand feelings
But I feel them all

Neurodivergency is not a problem
But the world is not made for us

Whenever things get particularly bad
I have the urge to scratch myself

My face, my arms, my legs

As if they weren't mine
As if I'm trying to escape this meat sack

I can't escape
Not like that

It's to easy to drink one glass
One glass can't hurt
One glass isn't that much

I'm not an alcoholic
I don't even drink more than 7 glasses a week
But I still drink every day

I noticed
So I tried to stop
But as soon as I'm not paying attention

It's only one glass

I'm a giver
I try to give everyone a piece
But before I know it
There's nothing left of me

Please be patient with me
I'm trying to learn how to be
How to give
Without losing myself

So, if you ask me for a piece
Next time
Ask yourself how bad you need it
Because I may need it more

I used to be a wonderer
Questioning everything I learned
Seeking knowledge in all kinds of places

Now I'm still a wonderer
But my magic's gone

I need to be patient with myself
I'm sorry
Just give me some time
I'm trying

"Smile! Why do you look so serious?"
Is what I heard
I was about 15 or 16
He was a fully grown man

"Smile, it could never happen."
Is what they heard
They were aged 10 to 60+
He was a fully grown man

We don't owe you a smile
Not since you stole it
You stole so much from us
Our innocence, our happiness, our autonomy

We won't smile for you
You don't deserve it

Why are you so angry? He asks
I am not angry, I reply
Or am I?
I don't know

Why did I raise my voice?
I only meant to say how I feel
But I guess that's the problem
I don't know

I don't mean to be angry
I don't mean to yell
I just don't have control
My voice has a life of its own

They call it voice regulation
It's something I lack
It's not that I don't want to
It's just that I can't

I'm not angry
I'm not sad
I'm just being me
And I'm sorry if I hurt you

All I've loved

He carried pain from many years
Withered
Gray, lost, and ready to let go

I could feel everything
And yet
I was just a bystander

I kept him close
Here, he was safe
Our bed
Carrying shared memories, feelings, love,
And
Our beings

He embraced me
Kept me safe and warm
But as I held his hand
I felt his breath calm
Slow
And Sleeping

You're safe now

He was inside me when I woke
Pain radiating through my body
I cried

He said

I moaned so I must have enjoyed it
I guided his hand in my sleep
He was sleeping too
It couldn't have been his fault

Why are you crying, he asked
I didn't do it on purpose

When I left his house that day
I felt guilty

I was seventeen
He went with me to the hospital
The operation went smooth

We got home
He asked for sex
I declined
I had just had an operation there

Well, he said
You've been anaesthetized
I declined
He got mad at me and left

I felt guilty

It was graduation
We were broken up
He was in my room
I was getting ready

He wanted sex
I did not

We argued
He pushed the buttons I had
I gave in and laid down on my bed
Let him do his thing
I tried to ignore the pain

Graduation was good
I was happy because I had forgotten
What had happened before

-    Is this what love is?

I'm standing in the kitchen
He comes up behind me

Wraps his arms around my waist
Leans forward
And whispers in my ear
Do you want to go to the bedroom?

I'm sorry, I say
I'm not feeling it

Don't apologize, he answers
It's okay
I love you

He hugs me tight
Kisses me on the cheek
And goes to do his thing

-    This is what love is

The way you look at me melts away all my doubts about
your love for me

-    Thank you

As I open my eyes
I see you sleeping calmly besides me
The sound of your breathing fills the room

I smile as I drift back to sleep
This is where I was meant to be

I was never quite good at looking at you
Especially when you were naked
I always averted my eyes

I guess it was my body's way of letting me know we were
not meant to be

I was in Crete
A gut feeling startled me
I texted you, asking if you were okay
You replied that everything was fine

When I returned
You begged me to make love to you
Even though I wasn't feeling it
I was on my period, you know

After you fucked me
Left me sore
You said it
I have something to confess

You broke my trust
My self-respect
You used me, my body for pleasure
Because you knew it was off-limits if you had told me
before

It took years
Even after our breakup
For me to fully trust again

Even now I have moments of doubts
Phantom gut feelings
A read message without reply
Or arriving home late without notice

You took something from me
And I will never fully heal

You know
We had our good moments too

Smoking weed late at night in your friend's backyard
Picnicking on your uncles plot of land
Sailing just before a storm with pancakes after

I'm grateful for those moments
You used to be my friend
Then lover
Then nothing

I miss my friend
But it's better this way

For just a moment
I thought it was like before

Us being friends
Having fun together

But it was not the same
You loved me
And probably still do

You got upset by my engagement
While I happily talked with your girlfriend

I want you to know that it's okay
It's okay to let go

We were not meant to be
And you deserve to be happy

You told me I shouldn't work towards happiness
Because there isn't such a thing
But my happiness may not be what it means to you

My happiness is to be able to enjoy my body
No matter what I weigh
To write books and poems when I desire
Working on expanding my ever-growing garden

My happiness is being able to face the challenge
With hope rather than to break down and cry
To be able to work through rainy days
Instead of wishing I were gone

My happiness is knowing it will get better
Even when I have a bad day
To know that it will work out in the end
Without the fear that it won't work at all

My happiness is enjoying the sunlight
While I walk towards the grocery store
To feel the pain in my muscles after an exhausting day
And knowing that I did well

My happiness is making up after a fight
And giving each other the space we need
To give you a kiss on your cheek
As we go about our day

My happiness is not a fantasy
or a mere dream
My happiness is what people without depression call
Everyday life

The way your hands can't stop touching me
When I show you my body
Gently, yet lustful
That's the way that makes me love myself a little more

I love when you've drunk a little too much
And you're telling others how much you love me
Telling me how lucky you feel to have me

I love how I help you get into bed
Put a bucket next to your bedside, just in case
And watch you doze off contently

I love how you feel embarrassed by it
How, in those moments, you seem truly happy
Even though it only happens twice a year

I love you

Sometimes I notice how you jerk awake from a
nightmare
And I notice how you grab me tight
Afraid I would not lay next to you

I notice your body calming down
As you quickly drift off again
Holding me ever so tight

When I'm lying on my back
With your hands wrapped around my neck
I will look at you and whisper
"I love you"

- Our love is lustful and intense

Open windows
Crickets chirping
Thunder rumbling in the distance

Tear drops hitting the pillow
Confusion and anger dominating the room
Is this what I want?

Thinking of the past
The good, the bad

Longing for the future
For clarity, freedom

You were content
A homebody
Wanting to spend the rest of our lives together

I wanted more
To explore
Both myself and the world

I did not know
Was this my future?

More arguments followed
Threats, accusations, defeat

We were in your room
Supposed to talk about the situation
Solve it

I cried

I'm sure you did too
I was free

Sweat drips down your brow
As you thrust into me

Fan going high speed
As raspy screams leave my throat

I look into your eyes
They're filled with lust and desire

"I love you," I mouth
Your eyes widen and you thrust harder

Nails into your back
Your hands around my throat

"I love you," you say
And you release your love inside of me

Handle with care
I say as you ask me out

By agreeing to this relationship
You agree with the following terms and conditions

The moments filled with joy
Endless talks and laughter as I lay in your lap

Passionate love making
As if our bodies were made just right for each other

Soft reassurances
When you feel like you've lost your way

Silent tears
Filled with confusion and pain

Pushing you away
Because you deserve so much better

Destructive behavior
Both mentally and physically

Meltdowns and screaming late at night
As I'm desperately trying to understand my brain

Please handle with care
I know I'm not an easy person to be with
But I promise you

I try

Girls

Girls with soft lips and long lashes
Girls with long hair and cute dresses
Girls with dainty bodies and flawless skin

Girls with chapped lips and dark make-up
Girls with coloured hair and platform boots
Girls with chubby bodies and scars on their skin

Girls who used to be
Girls who want to be

I opened up to myself
And so much has changed

I opened up to myself
And I took me in with open arms

They say the eyes are a doorway to someone's soul
But I have to disagree

To see into someone's soul
Is to look into the small things in their live

The song they listen to when they are happy
The movies they watch when they are sad
Their artistic expression
Even if they claim not to have one

The tone at which they sing
And the lyrics they choose to vocalize
The way they dance in their room
When they think no one is watching

The face they make when they're concentrating
And the way their hands move when they talk
As if they spoke an entirely different language

The meal they like to eat
When it's been a long and hard day
Who they think of
When they're lonely late at night

The dreams they have
And the trauma they work through

Someone's soul can't be seen at once
You have to look at each piece
One by one
And find a beautiful creature in front of you

I remember my mom calling me to tell me the news
She was crying
And I did my best not to

She told me how proud she was
For choosing my happiness over convenience
For not conforming to the norm
For being myself

My parents had always tried to protect me
To choose the safe route
But I wasn't made for that
I can't pursue a goal without happiness

This was the moment she realized that it's okay
Okay not to follow the normal
And okay to choose happiness over security
It was the moment she realized I didn't need protection
But support

And I'm thankful for that

You lay still
As I trace my fingers over your body
From your jaw to your neck
All the way down

I kiss the stretch marks that tell their story
Twirl the little hairs that you decided to let grow
And caress you gently until you want more

All I'm becoming

She's nature
Flowers blossoming around her
Hands in the dirt
Quietly sitting in the yard
She is Green

She's sunshine
The warmth on her face
Child-like and genuine
Smiling as her freckles grow
She is Yellow

She's passion
Heat rising in her chest
Balled fists and tears
Battling injustice
She is Red

She's mystic
Speaking to the wild
Drawing sigils and spells
Honoring the gods
She is Purple

She's serene
Diving into the deep end
Holding her breath
Watching as the world passes by
She is Blue

She's quiet
Emotionless and cold
Unable to feel

And no intention to do so
She is Grey

She's restless
Broken down, laying on the ground
A head full of thoughts
But not understanding a single one
She is all colors at once

I was never good at understanding my feelings
But I do understand tears

Tears from passion
Flowing from my eyes as I speak about the things I fight
for

Tears from happiness
When I image the place my heart longs for

Tears from beauty
When I hear music that speaks to my heart

Tears from love
When I remember the ones that care about me

Tears from pain
When the world becomes too much to bear

Tears from confusion
When the words from my mouth are different from the
ones in my heart

Tears from sadness
When I feel the pain of our suffering

My feet can't wait to feel the ground
made up of sticks
dirt and the core of its spirits

I want to become one
feel the peace
wander around
sleep in the moss and befriend the deer

I want to starve
my body slowly turning part of the forest
in which my spirit will wander forever

Guiding other lost souls

I must have been 16
Maybe 15
When Iceland first called to me
From then on, it was a goal

Some nights I cried
The need to leave was too much
Other nights I longed
For a place I had never been before

When the plane landed
I felt calm, peaceful
But when I stood there
In pure nature
I knew

I was home

Plants bring me peace
I lost count of the numbers
Taking care of them makes me calm
And they've adapted to my patterns
They fill the air with freshness
And make my home a little greener
Not just in the literal sense

I'm trying to fill my balcony
With plants as well
Edible plants, however
A start at being self-sufficient
I'm not very good yet
But the more I work
The more I feel in tune

When I am gone
I do not want you to mourn

Plant a tree in my name
Use my ashes to fertilize its growth
Spread the rest where I want to be

I am back where I belong

I miss the early morning walks
Mist above the lake
Birds chirping in harmony

The natural silence
A frog passing by my feet
As I dip my toes in the cold water

Petrichor entering my nose
Opening my senses
Warming my heart

Barefoot I walk over the grass
As ants and spiders shoot away
The dew covering my toes

Small shivers travel over my body
The cold air awakens me
Forming steam clouds as I laugh

I am happy

I am my illness

I am the overstimulated mind
Wanting to escape from the world

I am the quivering body
Trembling with unidentifiable emotions

I am the unstoppable panic attacks
Where nothing seems to calm me down

I am my illness
Yet I am so much more

I am the unwavering curiosity
Looking to learn more every day

I am the boundless creativity
Finding new ways to express myself

I am the unconditional empath
Wanting to help in every way I can

I am my illness
And that's okay

I was a girl
I played with barbies and dinosaurs
I dressed as princesses and the knights who saved them
I enjoyed make-up and video games

I was a girl
I wore twirly dresses and cargo shorts
I played hide-and-seek and in the mud
I loved cats and dogs and played with insects

I was a girl
I had long hair and cut it short
I loved boys and also girls
I shaved my armpits but wanted a moustache

I was a girl,
Or so I thought

Nobody told me how
chopping my hair off
would make me feel so different

Nobody told me that
Wearing men's clothing
Would feel so comfortable

Nobody told me that
Writing about my feelings
Made me feel so validated

So I came out
And yet

Nobody told me that
Coming out
Would change me so much

Nobody told me that
I would want
To explore myself even more

Nobody told me that
This opened
A new chapter of my life

Waking up into a constant battle
To stay sane
To stay healthy
To work to better myself

There are days where I fail
And I long for a way out
Just not to exist anymore

Other days I succeed
Feeling euphoric
Only to dread the next day

Living is a constant battle
But I'm still fighting

My body is fueled by anger
Anger at injustice, racism, sexism
It helps me fight for the good cause

My body is fueled by compassion
Helping others and showing mercy
It helps me stay kind, even when I don't want to be

My body is fueled by curiosity
Always looking to learn more about the world
It helps me to stay informed and tolerant

My body is fueled by nature
And I know I will give it back eventually
I just hope that I can be meaningful in the meantime

I used to live my life
The way I thought people expected me to be

Now I try to live my life
The way I want it to be

And it's made me so much happier

Your reaction is normal, she spoke
But you'll have to accept it

But I don't want to accept it, I replied
If I have to live the rest of my life like this
Then I don't want to live at all

She sighed.

Look at all you've achieved
You're so young
It takes getting used to
But you will feel better

Your reaction is normal
It truly is
Your reaction is normal for an abnormal situation

And you know what?
She is right.

I don't like my body

My double chin
My inherited flappy arms

The belly that keeps getting pudgier
Or the fat-rolls on my back

The eczema on my hands
And the stretch-marks that keep growing

My ever itching nose
And my weirdly shaped butt

I don't like my body
But it's part of me
And it's provided me with life
So I guess I'll have to keep it

I'll try to like my body

I'm not afraid of dying
But I wouldn't want to miss the beauty of the world

The powerful storms,
Blowing away the sturdiest trees

The coldest days
Where the snow seems to fall non-stop

The deep forests
Where you're not sure what's real anymore

The wild sea
Harbouring creatures we haven't even discovered yet

I want to learn
To see
To feel

So no,
I'm not afraid of dying
But I hope it will be a little while

Sometimes I feel like I don't belong
That this vessel isn't mine

I don't belong in the city
But in the forest

Not in this life
But free, eternal growth

Rhizomatic growth
Being everything and nothing at once

It's okay not to be okay
It's okay to be sad
To be depressed
Angry
Powerless

We're all so focused on producing
That we forget to take care of ourselves

So be angry
Cry your eyes out
Scream, punch, fall apart

You will rebuild yourself
And you will be stronger
More resilient
And ready to take on the world

My body isn't perfect
But she's the only thing I have

Sometimes I hate her
Her small rolls and dents

Her red spots that won't stop itching
And the pitch black hairs that grow in places they're not
supposed to

Still, life's too short to hate yourself
So, I try to love my body a little bit more

It's not easy
But step by step, I feel myself changing
My heart filling with love

There's something magical about
The nights where the wind is as silent as an owl
Where the water seems to be ice

No birdsong in the distance
Just the pure air
The stars
And you

Inhale the magic
Make it your own

Sometimes I just cannot give anymore
My brain is stuck, my body is tired, and my heart is sore
No energy left to care for myself
I gave it my all, and I'm left with none

Empathy is a blessed curse
A disease made of love and kindness
I try so hard to give it my all
But forget myself in the process

I've tried being unkind
I've tried to stop understanding
But I can't
It's in my blood

That's okay
I need to learn

I look in the mirror and sigh
Grab my soft belly
And wiggle it around
This used to be flat

I remind myself of what "used to" was
"Used to" was when I was still a child
With a developing body
And without the pressure of adulthood

And even then
As a child
I used to think that I was too fat
All because my organs needed space

So, yes, I am soft
I am chubby and my belly wiggles
But I am a whole person
With beauty, strengths, and passion

I've had my fair share of emotional issues
Being unable to function in a capitalistic world
Where your body is somehow still equal to your worth
Rather than your abilities

I may not love myself now
But I will be damned if I don't try
Because for someone to hate themselves because of
their body
Is something no one should go through

I got a garden this year
And I was so excited to start
But like most things when you start
It's not going as perfect as I'd hoped

I like to think of my garden as a metaphor
A metaphor for my mental health
Because like a garden
Your mental health needs care too

So, there may be some flourishing trees and bushes
But there's also the slug infestation that keeps eating
new sprouts
And while there's plenty of wildlife around
Some can harm you if you let them get too close

Some plants may wilt
While others may thrive
I care for them equally
But sometimes that's just how it is

I learn a lot while I'm gardening
About what works and what doesn't
And I know I won't be too successful in the first year
But I can use my knowledge for the coming years

And believe me,
I will thrive

Thank you